THE ULTIMATE BEGIN
DRUM BASICS
STEPS ONE & TWO COMBINED

MIKE FINKELSTEIN   SANDY GENNARO   JOE TESTA

CONTRIBUTING EDITOR:
SANDY FELDSTEIN

Sandy Gennaro, author and artist of the UBS Drum Basics Videos 1 and 2, is currently a faculty member at the Drummers Collective in New York City. He has recorded and toured with the following artists: Michael Bolton, Cyndi Lauper, Joan Jett and The Blackhearts, Johnny Winter, The Monkees, Little Steven Van Zandt, Pat Travers Band, Robin Gibb, The Mamas and Papas and Peter Noone.

Special Thanks to Sandy Feldstein and David Hakim for giving us the chance, and their support.

Sandy Gennaro would like to thank Ludwig Drums, Paiste Cymbals, Drum Workshop, Hot Sticks and Ray-Ban. He would also like to thank his wife Shari for her continued support and inspiration and, to his little girl Jeri, may the beat go on !!!

Editors/Project Managers: Mike Finkelstein and Joe Testa
Cover Layout: Joann Carrera
Technical Editors: Glyn Dryhurst and Albert Nigro
Engraver: Andrew Parks
Recorded Tracks: Julio Hernandez, Lee Levin, Mike Levine, and Daniel Warner at Down-Time Studios
Interior Photography: Gail M. Hopkins

CONTENTS

Contents   Page No.   (CD Track)

INTRODUCTION

In this book you will learn:
- About the drum set
- The drummer's role in a band
- How to hold the sticks
- How to play basic beats
- Rock beat variations
- Note values
- Song structure and the drummer's role in a song
- How to play drum fills
- Warm-up exercises

No matter what style you play, the drummer's role is to be the heartbeat and the foundation of the music. Similar to learning how to ride a bike, once you learn the basic fundamentals you never forget them. This book will give you the vocabulary necessary to allow you to grow to what ever levels you would like to achieve.

It isn't necessary to own a drum set to take full advantage of this book. Actually, all you need is a pair of sticks and the desire to learn.

THE BASS DRUM

Range: The drum set contains a wide range of sounds. To build from the bottom (low range) to the top (high range) we start with the bass drum. In most music, the bass drum locks in with what the bass guitar is playing.

CD
(**1**) (Listen to the bass drum, with and without the bass guitar)

Explanation and Position: The bass drum is played with a bass drum pedal which is operated by the foot. Position your seat height so your thighs are parallel to the floor. The front of the drum may be slightly elevated to allow better sound projection.

How to Play: There are two basic techniques for playing the bass drum:
1) Heel Down: Your foot remains flat on the foot pedal. Power and control come from the ankle. Use the same action as tapping your foot on the ground.

 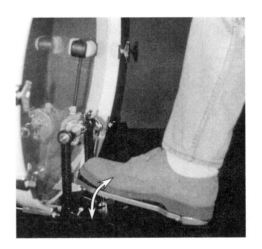

2) Heel Up: The ball of your foot is placed on the widest part of the pedal. The entire leg is used in conjunction with the toes to achieve better control and power.

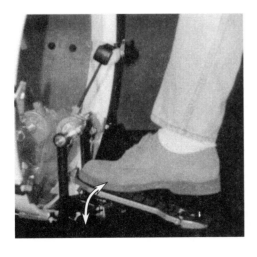 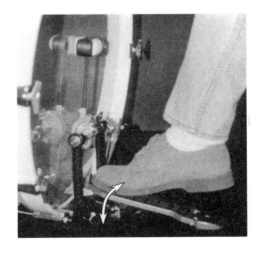

How well you play is based on how relaxed you are. Being relaxed means being comfortable. You should experiment to find what is best for you.

Lesson 1

CD 2 a) Listen to the music without the bass drum.

CD 3 b) Now listen to the music with the bass drum. Listen to what the bass drum adds to the music.

c) Begin by counting: 1 & 2 & 3 & 4 &

d) Count and play the circled numbers with right foot on the bass drum.

① & ② & ③ & ④ &

On our drum graph, it would look like this:

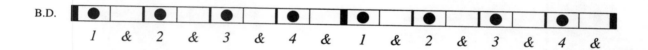

CD 4 e) Now count and play with the music.

THE SNARE DRUM

Range: The snare drum sound is the mid range of the set. It differs from the rest of the drums because there are wire snares that rest against the bottom head. When the top head is played, air is forced through the drum causing the bottom head and the wire snares to vibrate. This creates the snare drum's unique sound.

Grip: There are two types of grips:

1) Matched Grip: Both hands are held in the same way. Grip the stick between the second knuckle of the index finger and thumb one-third of the way up from the butt end. This prevents the stick from sliding and gives you control. The remaining fingers wrap lightly around the stick. The wrist and fingers should be in line with the forearm so that the stick becomes a natural extension of the arm.

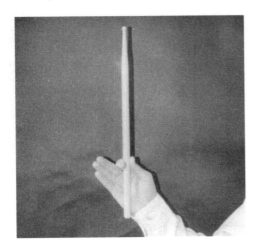 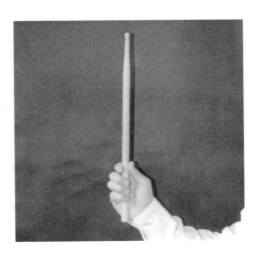

2) Traditional Grip: The right hand holds the stick in the matched grip style. The left hand, however, is held in a completely different way. The stick is held in the webbing of the hand between the thumb and index finger, approximately 1/3 of the distance from the butt end. The ring finger and pinky are under the stick, while the middle and index finger are on top of the stick.

Explanation and Position: The position of the drum depends on the type of grip used by the player. No matter what grip you use, your stroke should be the same. The drum should be placed between your legs, not too high or low. Be careful not to position the drum so that your hand hits your thigh. When using matched grip, the drum should be flat or slightly tilted downward toward the player. With the traditional grip, the drum may be slightly tilted downward to the right.

How to Play: The stroke for the right hand is very similar to casting a fishing rod or cracking a whip. Strike the drum with the tip of the stick a little off center.

The rebound should be quick as if the drum were a hot stove and the stick was your hand. The idea is to get the stick off the drum as quickly as possible. This will allow the head to vibrate fully and produce the best sound.

5 Practice counting and playing the circled numbers. Alternate right (R.H.) and left (L.H.) hands.

       ① & ② & ③ & ④ &
       R   L   R   L

Rim Shot: Another stroke used very often is the rim shot. A rim shot is created when the stick strikes the rim of the drum and the head of the drum at the same time.

 6 Listen to the difference between the regular stroke and the rim shot.

Lesson 2

 7 a) Listen to the music with the bass drum and no snare drum.

 8 b) Now listen to the music with the bass drum and snare drum. Listen to what the snare drum adds to the music.

c) Begin by counting: 1 & 2 & 3 & 4 &

The snare drum is played on the 2 and 4. This is known as the backbeat.

d) Count and play the circled numbers with your left hand.

      1 & ② & 3 & ④ &
              L   L

e) Now count and play this snare and bass drum pattern.

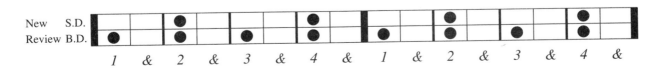

 9 f) Play Lesson 2 with music.

THE CYMBALS
(HI-HAT, RIDE AND CRASH)

Range: The high end sounds of the drum set are produced by the cymbals.

Hi-Hat Cymbals

Explanation and Position: The hi-hat consists of two cymbals that are mounted on the hi-hat stand.

The hi-hat stand contains a rod which goes through the hollow stand. It connects with the foot pedal. (The foot movement on the pedal dictates the up and down movement of the rod.)

The bottom cymbal is placed upside down on the felt pad of the stand.

The top cymbal is attached to the rod with a clutch which you tighten with a wing nut. The cymbals should be 3/4" or an inch apart. When the foot pedal is pressed, the cymbals come together to make a "chick" sound.

The hi-hat should be positioned just left of the snare drum. Not too high or low, and not too forward or back.

CD
(10) (listen to the hi-hat chick)

How to Play: There are two ways to play the hi-hat cymbals: with your foot or hands.
1) Hi-Hat with Foot: There are two basic techniques for playing the hi-hat with your foot.
a. Heel Down: Your foot remains flat on the foot pedal. Power and control come from the ankle.

b. Heel Up: The ball of your foot is placed on the widest part of the pedal. The entire leg is used in conjunction with the toes to achieve better control and power.

Lesson 3

CD
(11) a) Listen to the music with the bass drum and snare drum.

CD
(12) b) Now listen to the music with the hi-hat added. Listen to what the hi-hat adds to the music.

c) Begin by counting: 1 & 2 & 3 & 4 &

d) Count and play the circled numbers with left foot on the hi-hat. (Practice both the heel up and heel down technique):

1 & ② & 3 & ④ &

e) Now count and play the new hi-hat pattern with the snare and bass drum pattern. Note: The hi-hat is indicated on the drum graph with an "X" in its assigned box. Also practice playing the hi-hat on all four beats.

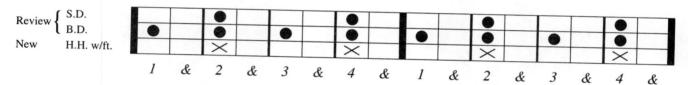

Review { S.D.
B.D.
New   H.H. w/ft.

1 & 2 & 3 & 4 & 1 & 2 & 3 & 4 &

CD
(13) f) Play Lesson 3 with music.

2) Hi-Hat Played with the Stick: A common approach to playing the hi-hat is to keep the cymbals closed with the left foot while playing with a stick (right hand).

Lesson 4

 a) Listen to the music with the bass drum and snare drum.

 b) Now listen to the music with the new hi-hat pattern added. Listen to what the new hi-hat pattern adds to the music.

c) Begin by counting: 1 & 2 & 3 & 4 &

d) Count and play the circled numbers with the right hand on the hi-hat.

① ⓐ ② ⓐ ③ ⓐ ④ ⓐ

e) Now count and play the new hi-hat pattern with the snare and bass drum pattern. You will have to cross the right hand over the left hand.

Note: When the hi-hat is played with the stick, it will be indicated with a "X" on its assigned *line*.

Beat #1

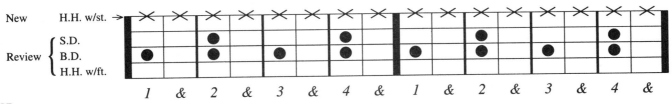

 f) Play Lesson 4 with music.

Ride Cymbal

Explanation and Position: The ride cymbal helps change the characteristic of the beat by bringing a brighter sound to the overall mix of the drum set. More often than not it is located to the right of the bass drum.

How To Play: There are many ways to play the ride cymbal. Each creates a different sound.

CD

(17) 1) Play the cymbal with the tip of the stick 1/3 of the way in from the edge. This will produce a "ping" sound.

CD

(18) 2) Play the cymbal with the shaft of the stick near the edge of the cymbal. This creates a broader sound.

CD

(19) 3) Play with the shaft of the stick on the bell to create an accented "ping".

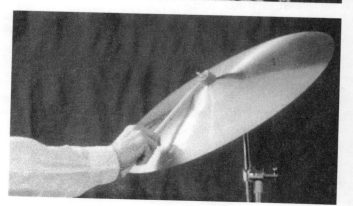

Lesson 5

CD 20 a) Listen to the music with the bass drum, snare drum and hi-hat (left foot).

CD 21 b) Now listen to the music with the new ride pattern added. Listen to what the new ride pattern adds to the music.

c) Begin by counting: 1 & 2 & 3 & 4 &

d) Count and play the circled numbers with right hand on the ride cymbal.

① ⟨&⟩ ② ⟨&⟩ ③ ⟨&⟩ ④ ⟨&⟩

e) Now count and play the new ride pattern with the snare and bass drum pattern. We'll also add the hi-hat pattern learned in Lesson 3. Note: The ride cymbal is indicated on the drum graph with an "X" in its assigned box.

Beat #2

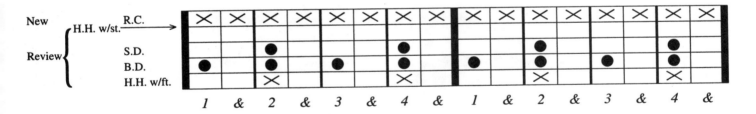

CD 22 f) Play Lesson 5 with music.

Crash Cymbal

Explanation and Position: One way to add excitement and high end to any given beat is to use crash cymbals. Like all cymbals, they come in different thickness and sizes to produce various tones. Their primary use is to emphasize and/or accent a certain musical phrase or idea. It is common to place a crash cymbal to the left of the bass drum.

CD 23

How To Play: Crash cymbals are played with a "sweeping" stroke with the shaft of the stick.

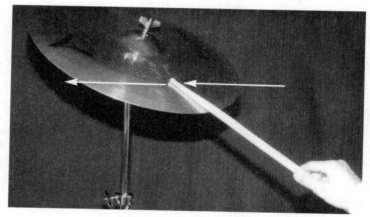

Lesson 6

CD 24   a) Listen to the music with the bass drum, snare drum and hi-hat (right hand).

CD 25   b) Now listen to the music with the crash cymbal added on beat 1. Listen to what the crash cymbal adds to the music.

c) Begin by counting: 1 & 2 & 3 & 4 &

d) Count and play the circled numbers with the right hand on the crash cymbal.

(1)   &   2   &   3   &   4   &

e) Now count and play adding the crash cymbal to BEAT #1. Note: The crash cymbal is indicated on the drum graph with a "X" on its assigned *line*. We'll call this BEAT #3.

Beat #3

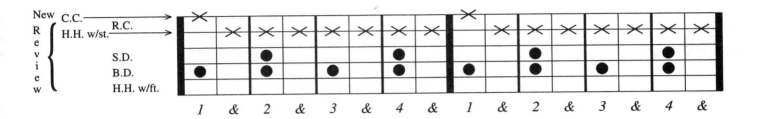

CD
26 f) Play Lesson 6 with music.

Lesson 7 (a variation on Lesson 6)

We can also add the crash cymbal on 1 of BEAT #2. We'll call this BEAT #4.

Beat #4

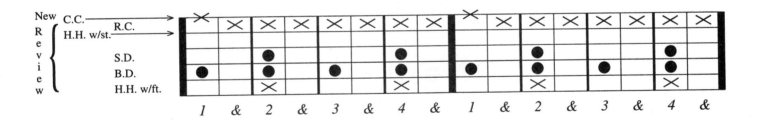

CD
27 Play Lesson 7 with music.

Lesson 8

PUTTING ALL FOUR BEATS TOGETHER:

We've added a bit of music to play along with. The object of this exercise is to play each beat *four* times and immediately go on to the next one.

CD 28 First listen to the example. Listen to how the beat works with the music.

CD 29 Now practice each beat in succession like the example.

Beat #1

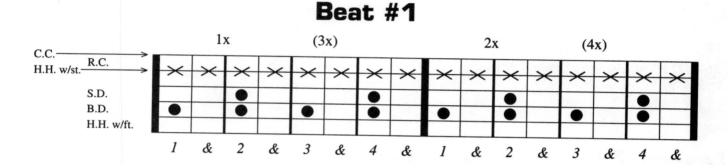

Beat #3

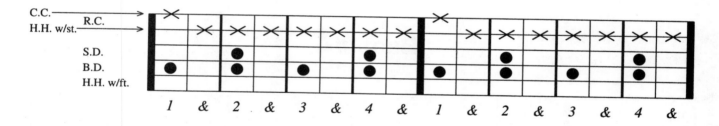

Beat #2

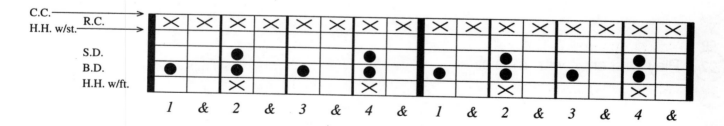

Beat #4

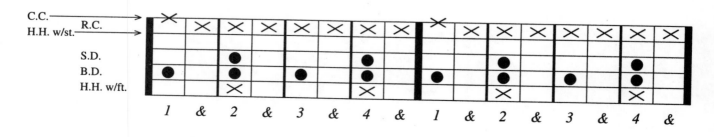

TEMPO

You can play any beat at different speeds. These different speeds are called tempos. Different tempos give the beat a whole new feel and it can change the characteristic of the beat.

CD
(30) While practicing each tempo concentrate on keeping steady time. Play Lesson 8 [page 18] at the new *slower* tempo.

CD
(31) Now play Lesson 8 at the *medium* tempo.

CD
(32) Play at the *fast* tempo.

DYNAMICS

You can play any beat at different volumes. These different volumes are called dynamics. Different dynamics create excitement within the music and it can bring new life to a simple beat.

Now take Lesson 8 and practice each dynamic. Be careful not to slow down when you play quietly or speed up when you play loudly.

CD
(33) Play at the *quiet* dynamic.

CD
(34) Play at the *medium* dynamic.

CD
(35) Play at the *loud* dynamic.

Lesson 9

Here are eight beat variations to practice. The hi-hat (R.H.) and the snare drum (L.H.) remain constant while the bass drum changes. Play each exercise along with the CD track. The first two times you will play along with the beat, the second two times with just a click track. After you master each variation, practice each beat on your own with a click (metronome and/or drum machine). Remember to practice each beat at various tempos and dynamics.

1)

CD
(36)

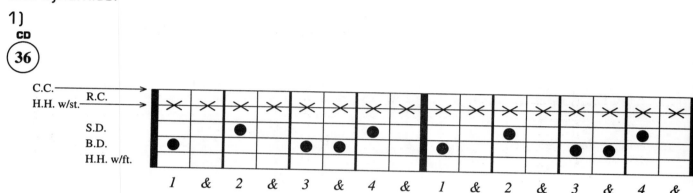

2)

CD
(37)

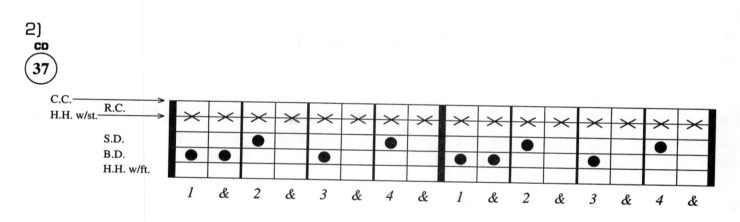

3)

CD
(38)

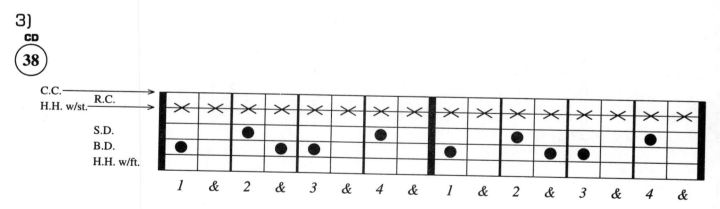

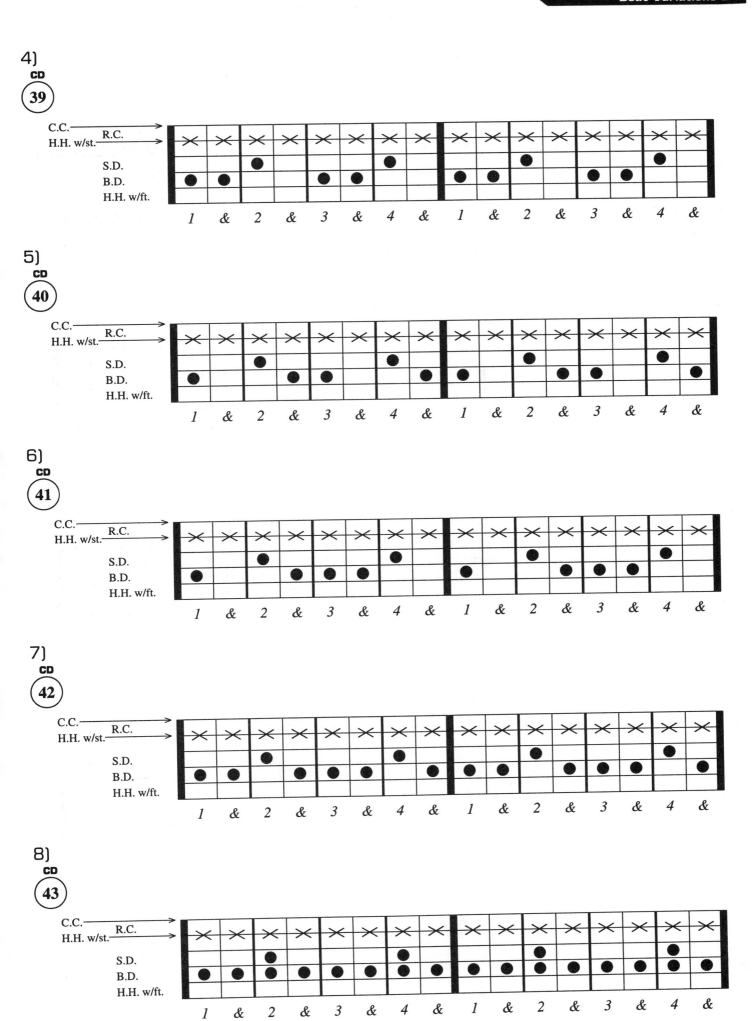

THE TOM TOMS

Range: Tom toms are predominately used for fills, so their range varies from high to low. There are two types of tom toms:

Explanation and Position:

1) Rack Toms: These toms are mounted on top of the bass drum or on a stand that hangs over the bass drum. They are usually set up from high pitch to low pitch, left to right, the smaller toms being the higher pitched and the larger toms being the lower pitched.

2) Floor Tom: This is the biggest tom tom. It is set up to the right of the snare drum and can stand on legs or hang from a mounted stand.

CD
(44) Listen to the tom toms, starting high to low and back again.

Note: Regarding all the examples in Lessons 10 - 12, listen to the beat on its corresponding CD track. Immediately following the beat, you will hear just a click so that you can practice the beat on your own.

Lesson 10

CD 45 Now play BEAT #2 and add (with your left hand) the new high tom and snare patterns. We'll call this BEAT #5.

Beat #5

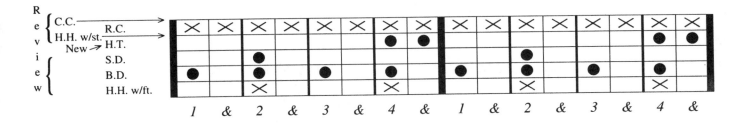

Lesson 11

CD 46 Now play BEAT #5 and play the new pattern on the floor tom instead of the high tom. This is BEAT #6.

Beat #6

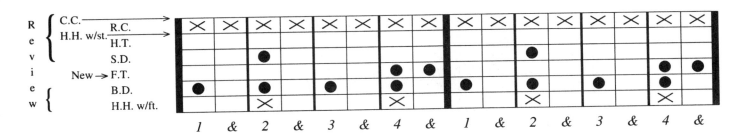

Lesson 12

CD 47 Now play BEAT #6 and play the new pattern on the floor tom, but this time play the snare pattern on the high tom. This is BEAT #7.

Beat #7

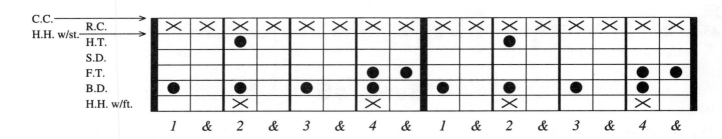

CD 48 Practice BEATS #5, #6 and #7 with the ride pattern on the hi-hat.

Beat #5 with H.H.

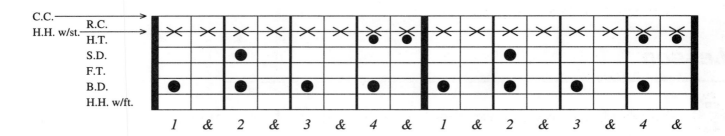

CD 49

Beat #6 with H.H.

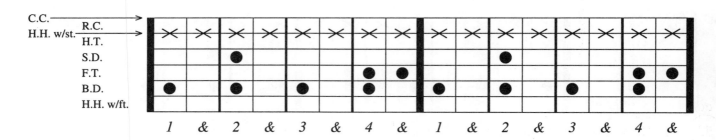

CD 50

Beat #7 with H.H.

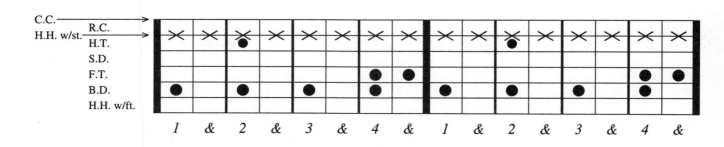

THE E's & THE A's:
A NEW WAY TO COUNT

Lesson 13

a) Play the following on the snare drum with just your right hand.

```
1   &   2   &   3   &   4   &
R   R   R   R   R   R   R   R
```

51 b) Play in between each right hand with your left hand (L). We will call all the "L's" the "e's" and the "a's".

```
1 (e) & (a)   2 (e) & (a)   3 (e) & (a)   4 (e) & (a)
R (L) R (L)   R (L) R (L)   R (L) R (L)   R (L) R (L)
```

c) Practice this same pattern on the hi-hat.

d) " 𝄎 " is called a repeat sign. When you see a repeat sign, repeat the pattern you just played.

52 e) Practice this pattern on the hi-hat with alternating strokes, but play every 2 and 4 on the snare drum with the right hand.

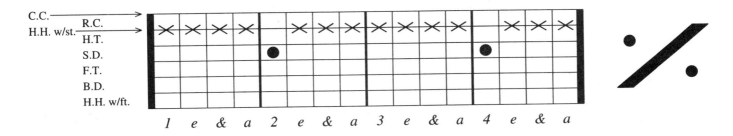

53 f) Now add the bass drum on the 1, 2, 3 and 4. We will call this BEAT #8. Once again, listen to the example and then play with the click.

Beat #8

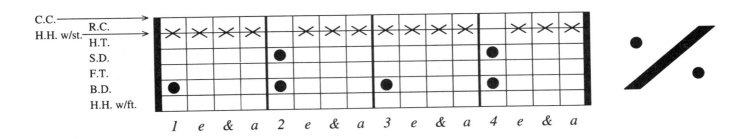

Lesson 14

You can practice different variations based on this groove. Here are two to listen to and then practice.

CD 54 1)

Beat #9

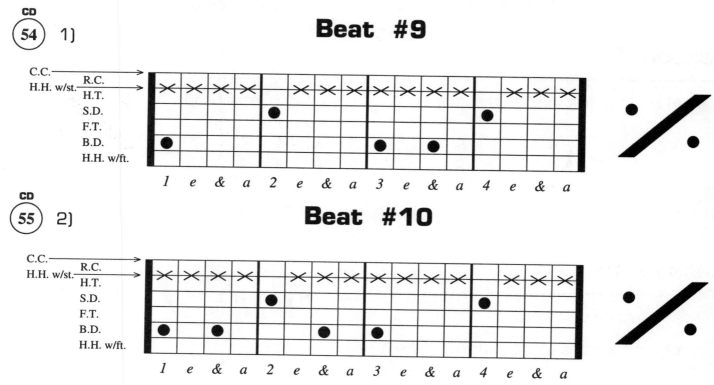

1 e & a 2 e & a 3 e & a 4 e & a

CD 55 2)

Beat #10

1 e & a 2 e & a 3 e & a 4 e & a

THE "TRIP" AND THE "LETS": ANOTHER RHYTHM

Lesson 15

a) Begin counting: 1 - Trip - Let - 2 - Trip - Let - 3 - Trip - Let - 4 - Trip - Let

CD 56 b) To get a feel for it, play with alternating sticking on the snare drum only.

1 Trip Let	2 Trip Let	3 Trip Let	4 Trip Let
R **L** R	**L** R **L**	R **L** R	**L** R **L**

c) Practice this same pattern on the hi-hat with just the right hand.

CD 57 d) Now practice the right hand pattern on the hi-hat, but play every 2 and 4 on the snare drum with the left hand.

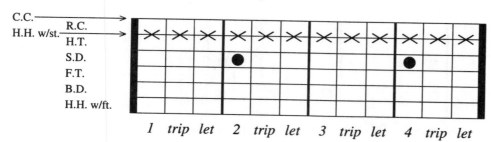

1 trip let 2 trip let 3 trip let 4 trip let

CD 58

d) Now add the bass drum on beats 1, 2, 3 and 4. We will call this BEAT #11. Listen to it and then practice with the click.

Beat #11

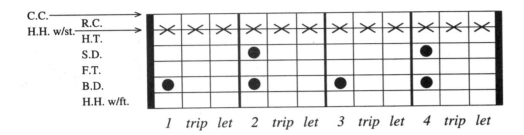 

Lesson 16

You can practice different variations based on this groove. Here are two:

CD 59

1)

Beat #12

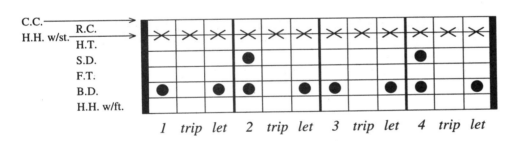 

CD 60

2)

Beat #13

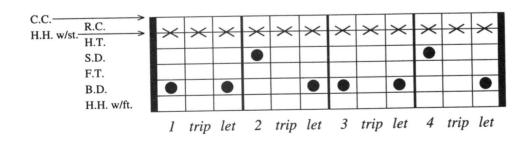 

INTRODUCING NOTE VALUES
(READING.... WHY?)

Lesson 17

Learning how to read expands your options in learning drum fills and beats. It also allows you to communicate with other instrumentalists and to become more creative.

At this point you already know how each drum relates to the musical staff. Look how the drum graph has prepared you to read music. It is perfectly related to the musical staff:

Drums

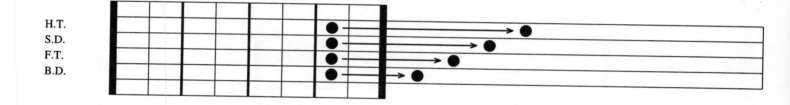

Cymbals

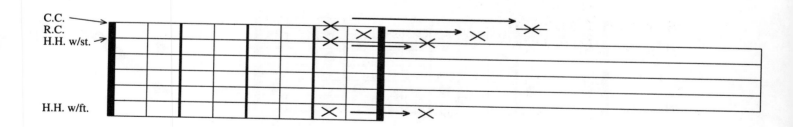

COUNTING NOTE VALUES AND RHYTHM

Lesson 18

Now that you understand how the drum graph relates to the musical staff, it is also important to know how the music is written on the staff. Without realizing it, you have already been reading basic notes and rhythms.

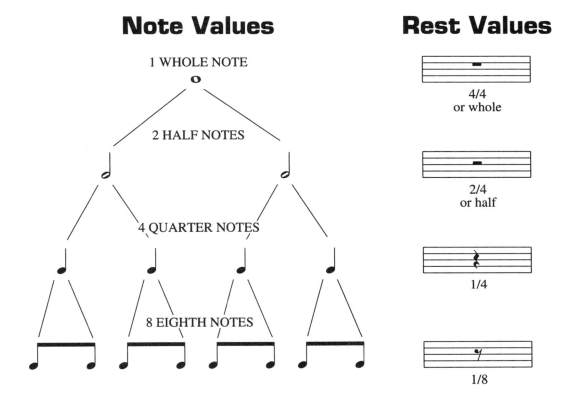

Since Lesson 1 you have been counting 1 & 2 & 3 & 4 &. The 1, 2, 3 and 4 are quarter notes and the "&'s" are eighth notes.

Eighth Notes can be divided into sixteenth notes.

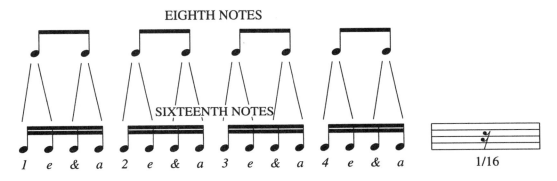

Notice you've been counting the "e's" and the "a's" since Lesson 13.

In Lesson 15 you learned what "Triplets" feel like. There are three eighth note triplets per one quarter note.

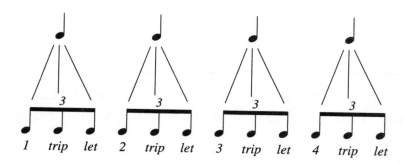

1 trip let 2 trip let 3 trip let 4 trip let

Notice the "1" "Trip" "Let" "2" "Trip" "Let" "3" "Trip" "Let" "4" "Trip" "Let" from Lesson 15.

MEASURES, BARLINES AND TIME SIGNATURES

Lesson 19

Music is divided into equal parts called measures. Barlines indicate the beginning and end of measures. A double barline, one thin and one thick, show the end of a piece.

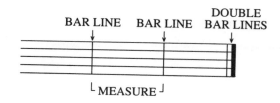

Time Signatures are placed at the beginning of a piece of music to show the number of beats (or counts) in each measure and the kind of note that receives one beat.

$\dfrac{4}{4}$ = four beats per measure
= quarter note gets one beat

Let's take a look at BEAT #1 and see how the drum graph translates into a bar of 4/4 in music notation.

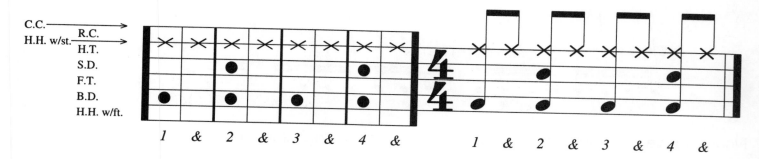

SONG FORM

Lesson 20

The primary function of a drummer is to play consistent time, but it is also important to support the form of the song. A basic song usually consists of three major sections: a VERSE, CHORUS and BRIDGE. There are many ways the drummer can support the song form. You can play different dynamics, variations of beats, or add drum fills.

Drum Fills: Drum fills are often used to lead the song from one section to the next. Listen to each example and how it sets up the musical change. Then play with the music on your own with only a click.

1-Beat Fills

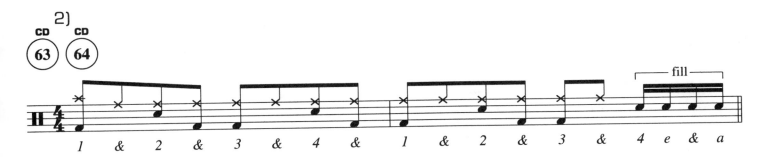

4)

5)

2-Beat Fills

6)

7)

PUTTING IT ALL TOGETHER

Now it's time for you to put all that you have learned to use. Play along with these next two tracks. The first is in a rock style, the second is a 12-bar blues. The CD will have two versions of each song, one with an example of the drum part and the other with a click so you can play along on your own.

ROCK PLAY ALONG

Chorus 2:

Bridge:

Gtr. Solo:

Chorus 3:

Chorus 4:

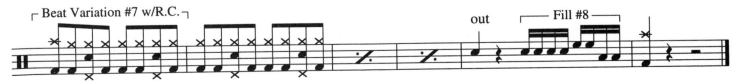

12-BAR BLUES PLAY ALONG

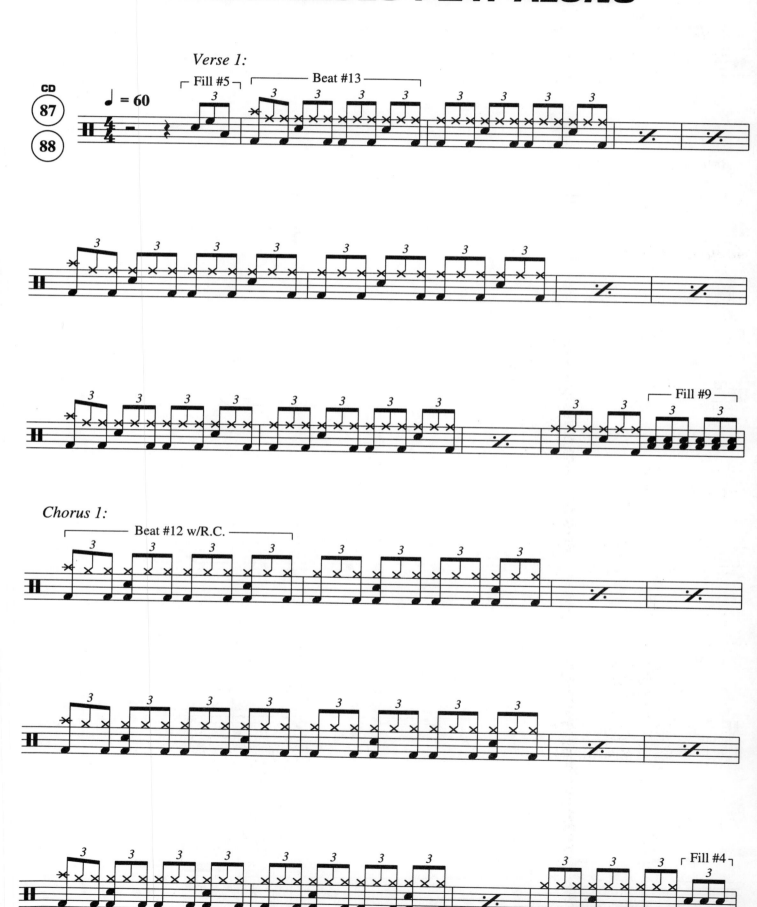

Solo 1 (Verse 2):

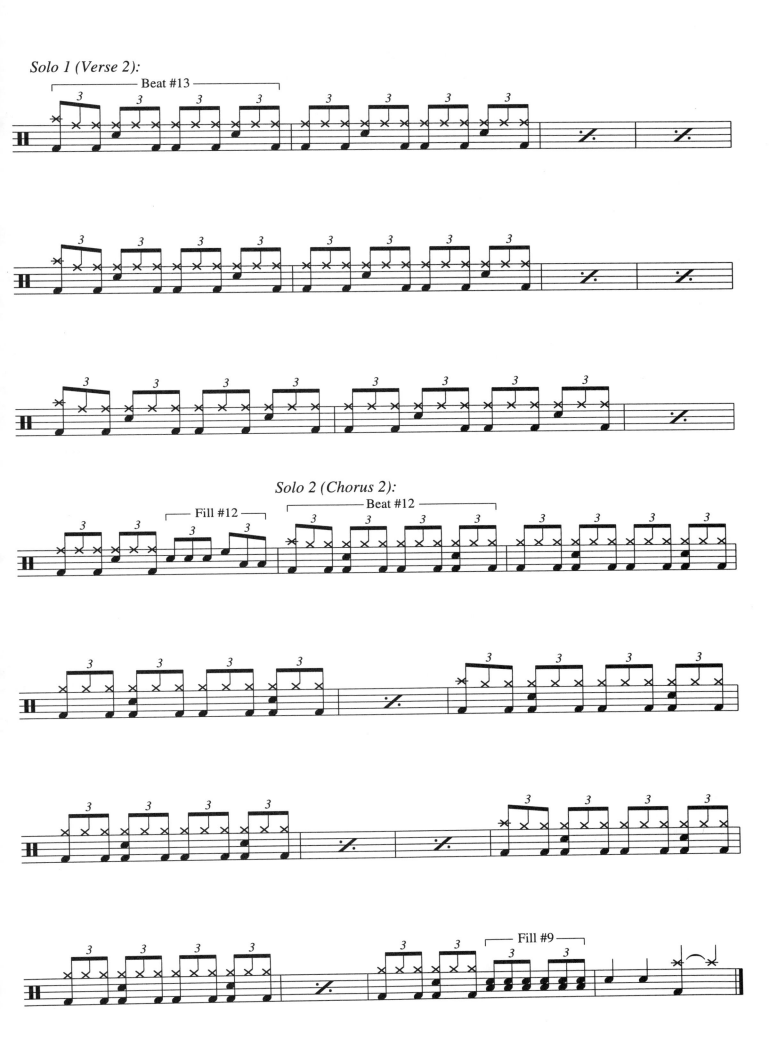

HAND WARM-UPS

Now that you know how to play the drums, here are some helpful exercises that will warm you up before playing. It is suggested that you practice all the warm-ups while playing the hi-hat on beats 2 and 4, and then on all 4 beats.

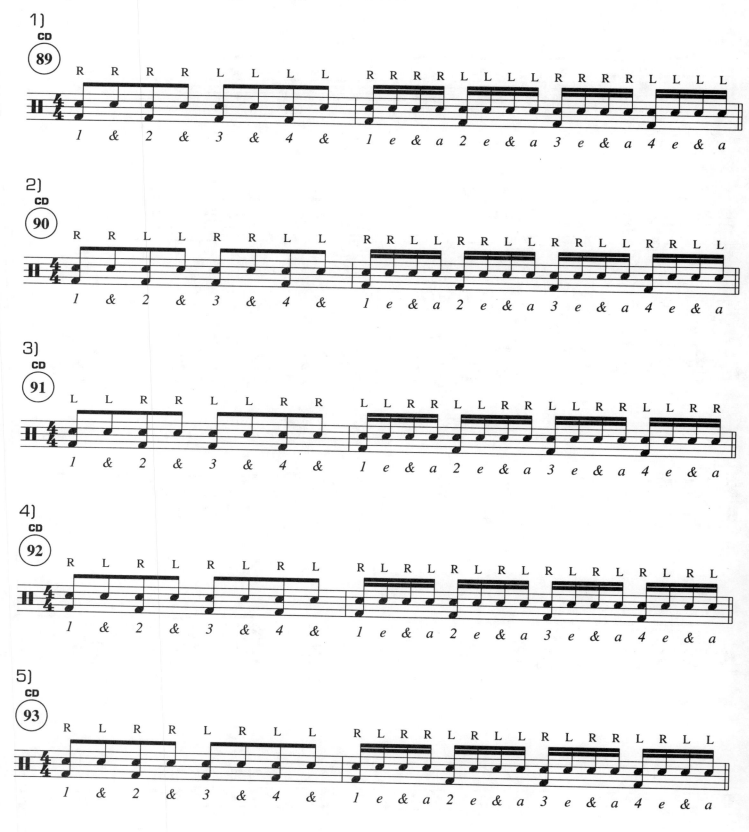

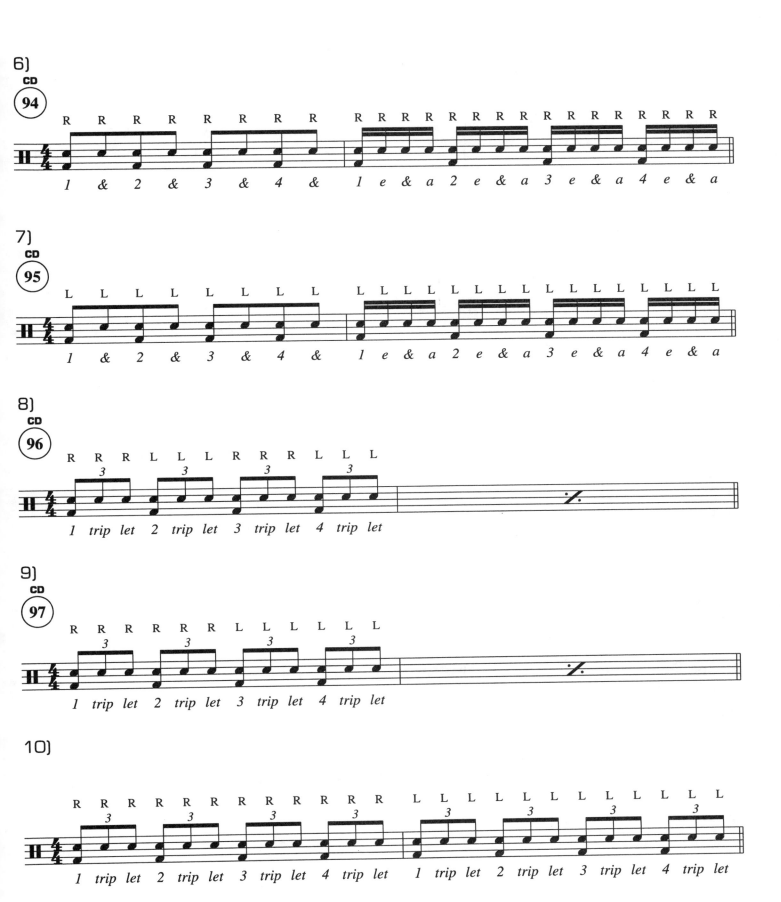

CONCLUSION

Congratulations! Now that you have learned the necessary musical vocabulary you can grow to any level you want. You can begin learning how to play drums in different musical styles. Use the ideas you have learned as a starting point to achieve the goals you set for yourself. Make up your own beats and fills while you practice and enjoy the instrument. Don't get discouraged if some things don't come as quickly as you would like. Remember you began playing to have fun! Be patient and go over troubled areas slowly until you have it mastered. The best source of learning is listening and playing with other musicians, so get together with some friends and create music!

If you enjoyed this book there are two other books in this series which focus on Rock and Blues playing:

In the Basic Rock Drums Book (UBSBK002CD) you will learn:
- Several new rock beats
- Great drum fills
- Practice tips
- Note values
- Creating a groove
- 16th note variations on the bass drum
- A rock ballad
- A rock shuffle
- Fill ideas for different grooves
- Use of the controlled open hi-hat
- A two beat pattern

In the Basic Blues Drum Book (UBSBK003CD) you will learn:
- Shuffles and slow blues grooves
- Alternate cymbal patterns for a shuffle
- Hi-hat coordination exercises
- Bass drum variations
- Blues Rhumba
- Open hi-hat sound
- The "Steve Gadd Shuffle"
- New fill ideas

All books are available through your local music dealers or
Note Service Music
P.O.Box 4340
Miami, FL
33014
1-800-628-1528 (ext 214 or 215)